Quilt Labels

by Barbara Baatz Hillman

The stories tied into our quilts are as dear to us as the beautiful creations themselves. Adding a handmade label to either a new quilt or an antique one is a simple and attractive way to ensure that important information about the quilt will be preserved for future generations.

Barbara Baatz Hillman, creator of *50 Nifty Iron-on Quilt Labels*, shares *50 more* of her wonderful label designs in this new book of easy-to-use iron-on transfers. A multitude of possibilities awaits quilters. The labels include designs for special occasions such as a wedding, new house, or new baby, as well as an abundance of charming motifs that are perfect for special gifts for family and friends.

Choose your favorite design, iron it onto fabric, then use a fine-point permanent marker to record important facts like who made the quilt, when and where it was completed, the person or occasion for whom it was created and, perhaps, the name of the design. Embellish with color, using crayons, markers, or embroidery, then turn edges under before blindstitching to the back of the quilt.

When giving a quilt as a gift, a label with a personal note will add an unforgettable touch.

Some of Barbara's labels provide space for adding the full story of your quilt or for later additions if the quilt is given away, published, exhibited, or wins an award. Even if the history of a quilt is a mystery, it's beneficial to record when and how you acquired it and why it is special to you.

A handmade label will add an heirloom finishing touch to your quilt and preserve the memories bound into your creation to be cherished for years to come.

Supplies

Light-colored fabric
Iron and ironing board
Freezer paper
Black fine-point permanent marker
Scissors

You may also need:

Crayons and/or permanent fabric markers
Kneaded eraser
Embroidery floss
Pressing cloth

Transferring the Design

Before transferring the design to your label fabric, follow steps 1 – 6, using a test transfer and scrap of label fabric to determine the best iron temperature and length of time needed for a good transfer.

1 Wash and dry fabric without using fabric softener.

2 Cut a piece of fabric 1" larger than printed design area. Cut fabric 3"– 4" larger than printed design area if you plan to add embroidery using a hoop.

3 Preheat iron using cotton setting; **do not** use steam. Because transfer ink may bleed through fabric, protect ironing surface with a clean piece of scrap muslin or paper.

4 Press fabric and allow to cool.

5 Cut away any unwanted words, test transfer, or page number before transferring the design.

6 Center transfer, inked side down, on right side of fabric. Place iron on transfer; hold for five seconds. Do not slide iron. Pick up iron and move to another position until entire design area has been pressed.

7 Carefully lift one corner of transfer to see if design has been transferred to fabric. If not, place iron on transfer for a few more seconds.

Personalizing Your Label With Crayons or Markers

To stabilize the fabric while embellishing your label, cut a piece of freezer paper the same size as your fabric. With iron set on a medium setting, press the shiny side of paper to the wrong side of your fabric. Allow to cool.

Tips for coloring with crayons

• Color all or just selected areas of the design with crayons. Begin by applying color sparingly and increasing pressure if stronger color is desired.

• Stray crayon flakes can be lifted from the fabric with a kneaded eraser.

• Heat set crayon colors by covering design with a pressing cloth and ironing using cotton setting.

• Custom colors can be created by applying one color, covering the design with a pressing cloth, ironing to set colors, then applying a second color.

• After coloring is complete, heat set a final time.

• Use the fine-point marker to enhance detail lines or outlines, if desired.

Tips for coloring with markers

• Always test markers on a scrap of label fabric; colors may be more intense or may bleed when used on fabric.

• If your quilt is to be washed, wash your test piece to check for colorfastness.

• When coloring adjacent areas of a design, allow each color to dry before adding next color.

• Follow manufacturer's instructions for drying time and heat setting ink, if needed.

• Use the fine-point marker to enhance detail lines or outlines, if desired.

See page 33 for finishing.

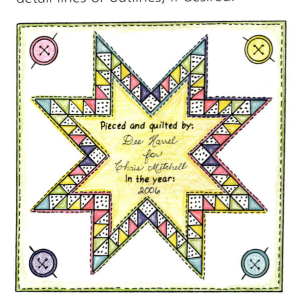

Personalizing Your Label
With Embroidery

Add an extra special touch to your label with embroidery stitches (see pages 34 – 35). Some suggested uses for the stitches include: Backstitches, Running Stitches, or Stem Stitches for lettering, outlining, and flower stems; Satin Stitches when a solid look is desired for berries, small leaves, and flower petals; French Knots for flower centers, small berries, and eyes; Lazy Daisy Stitches for small flower petals and leaves; Straight Stitches to add detail lines to small areas.

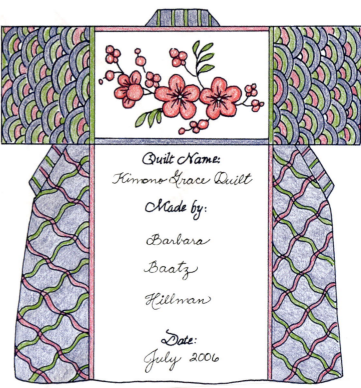

Quilt Name:
Kimono Grace Quilt
Made by:
Barbara
Baatz
Hillman

Date:
July 2006

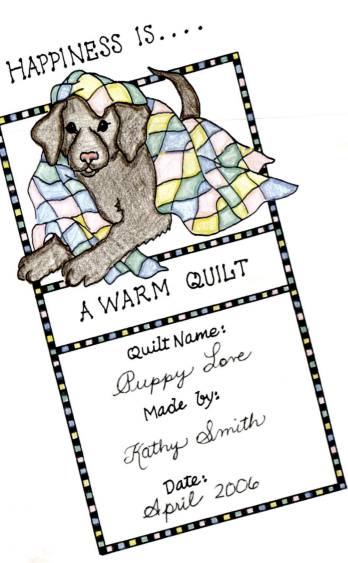

HAPPINESS IS....

A WARM QUILT

Quilt Name:
Puppy Love
Made by:
Kathy Smith

Date:
April 2006

• Before stitching with dark floss on light fabric, you may wish to set the floss color by soaking floss in a mixture of 1 tablespoon vinegar and 8 ounces of water. Allow floss to air dry.

• For most embroidery, we recommend using 3 strands of floss. You may choose to use 2 strands for a more delicate look or 4 strands for heavier coverage.

• Cut floss into 18" lengths. Floss this length does not fray or tangle as easily as longer lengths.

• Because the transfer ink is permanent, be sure stitches cover all transfer lines.

When life gives you scraps... Make a quilt!

Made by:

Date:

Quilt Name:

Made by:

Date:

Quilt Name:

5

Test Transfer

Quilt Name:

Made by:

Date:

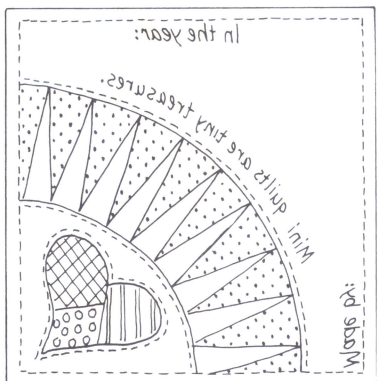

In the year:

Mini quilts are tiny treasures.

Made by:

Test Transfer

6

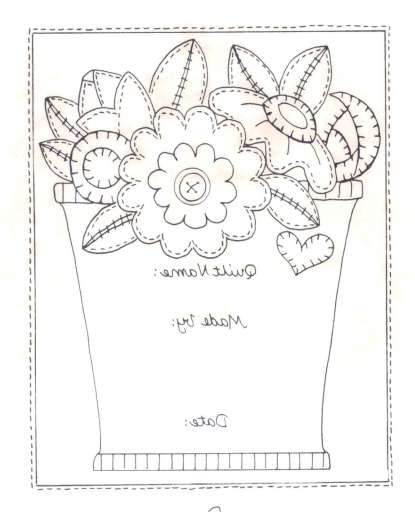

Test Transfer

Quilt Name:

Appliqued with love by:

Date:

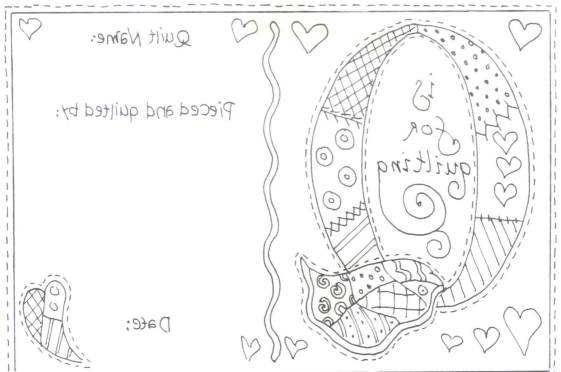

Quilt Name:

Pieced and quilted by:

Date:

Test Transfer

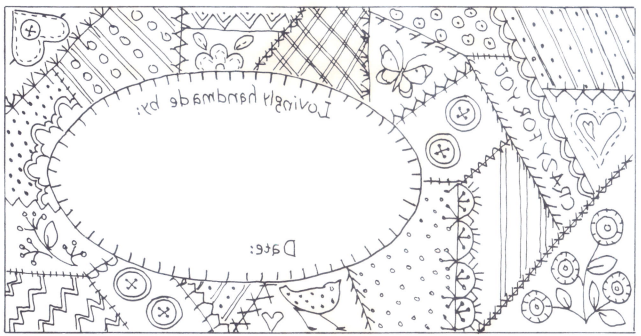

Test Transfer

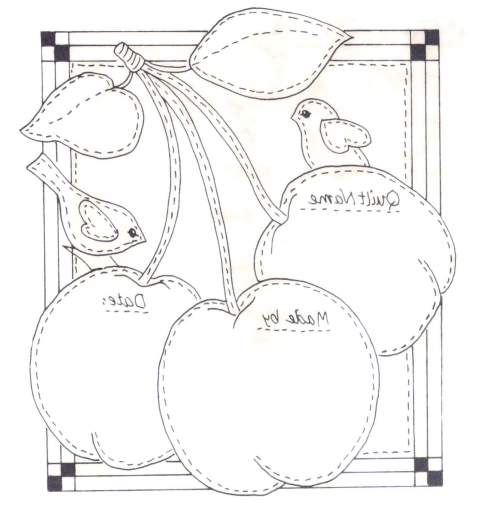

Test Transfer

Quilt Name:

A quilted token of friendship for:

Lovingly made by:

Date:

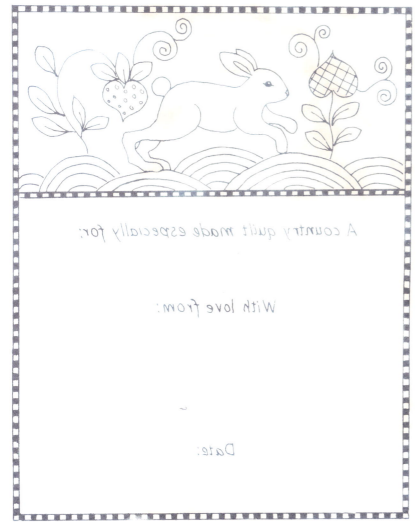

A country quilt made especially for:

With love from:

Date:

Test Transfer

Friendships
and quilts
are made
to be treasured

From the hand and heart of:

Date:

Handmade by:

Date:

Test Transfer

12

May this quilt forever be
A small remembrance of me.

Quilt Name:

Made by:

Date:

Quilted with memories of the friendship we've shared

Made with love for:

By:

Date:

Test Transfer

FROM MY HEART TO YOUR HOUSE

MADE FOR:

BY:

DATE:

An appliqued totem of friendship for:

Quilt Name:

Lovingly made by:

Date:

Test Transfer

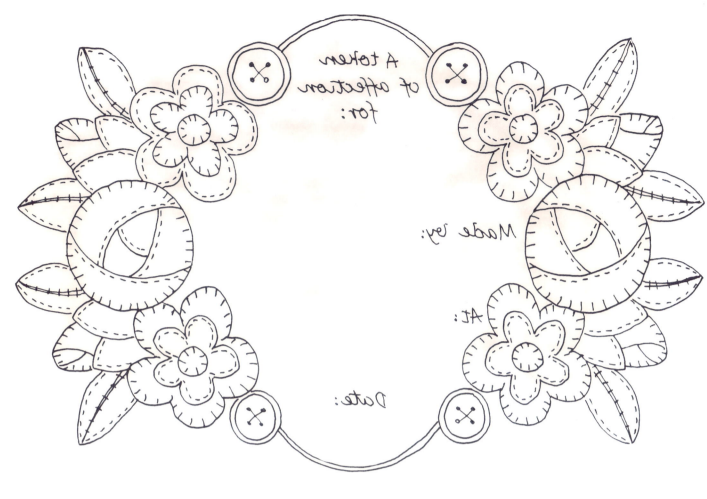

A token
of affection
for:

Made by:

At:

Date:

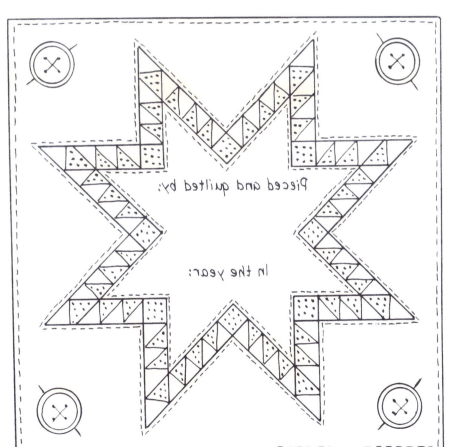

Pieced and quilted by:

In the year:

Test Transfer

Quilting.....It's a good thing

Quilt Name:

Appliqued and quilted by:

Date:

A quilted gift for a special friend

Quilted with love for:

by:

Date:

Test Transfer

Life is a quilt
sewn together
with memories.

Quilt Name:

Pieced and quilted by:

Date:

Test Transfer

17

Life is a quilt
sewn together
with memories.

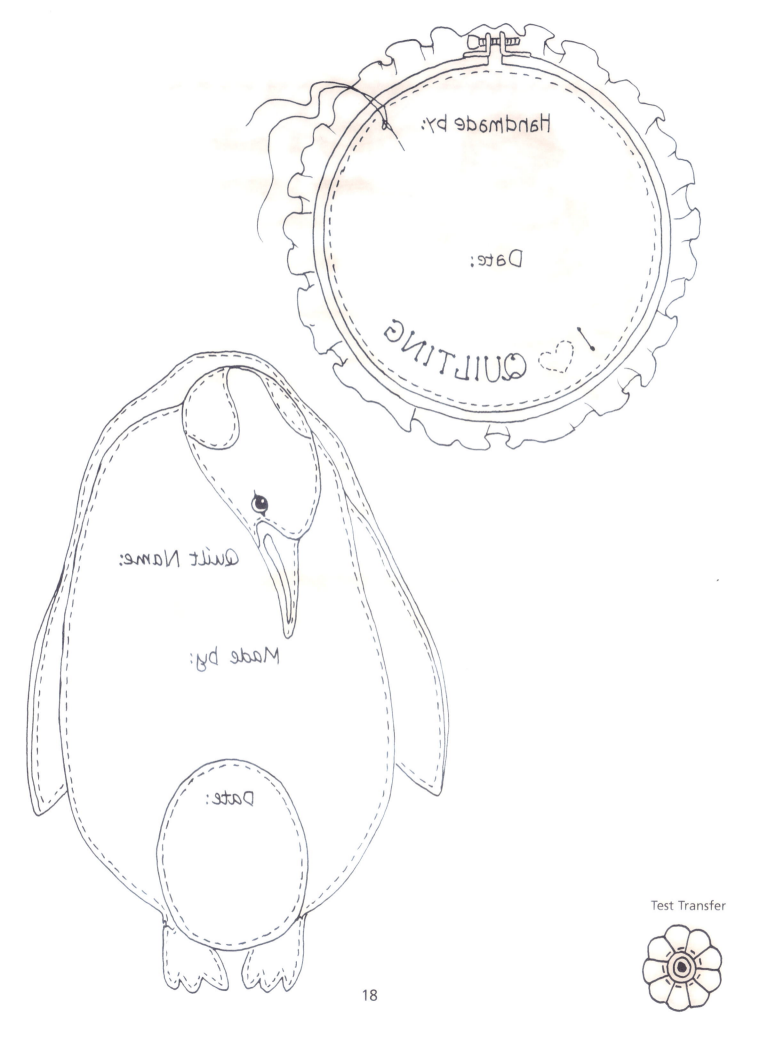

Handmade by:

Date:

I ♡ QUILTING

Quilt Name:

Made by:

Date:

Test Transfer

18

Test Transfer

A
Friendship
quilt
from all of us

To:

With love from:

In the year:

In the city and state of:

Test Transfer

*May your sorrows be patched
and your joys quilted*

A quilt for the
Bride and Groom

Made with love for:

In the year:

By:

Test Transfer

A QUILT FOR BABY

Quilt Name:

Made especially for:

With love from:

In the year:

Test Transfer

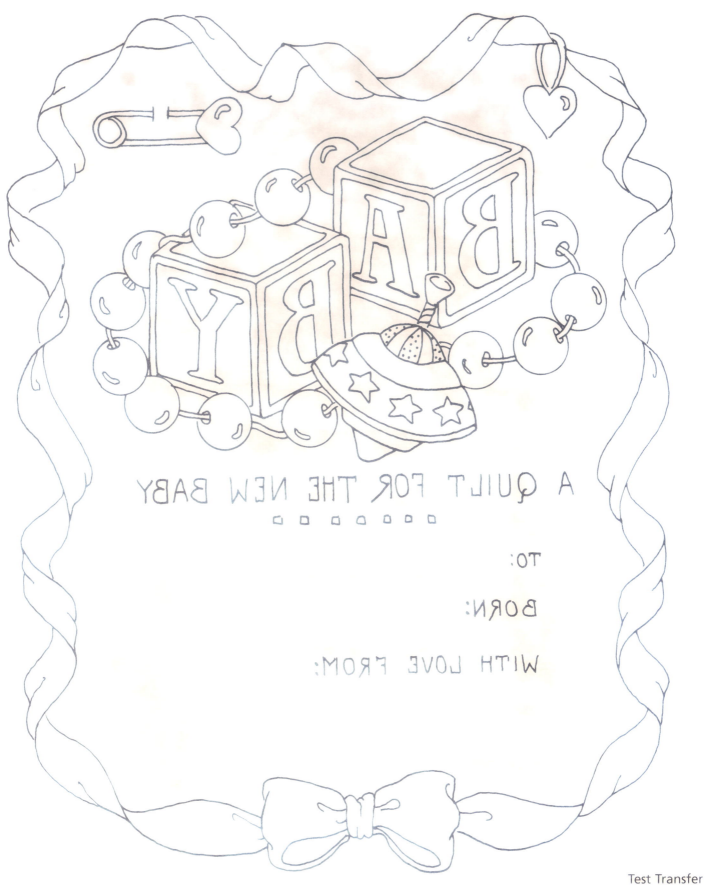

A QUILT FOR THE NEW BABY

TO:

BORN:

WITH LOVE FROM:

Test Transfer

For A Special
Boy

To:

With love from:

Date:

May this quilt forever be ~
A small remembrance of me.

Quilt Name:

Made by:

Date:

Test Transfer

24

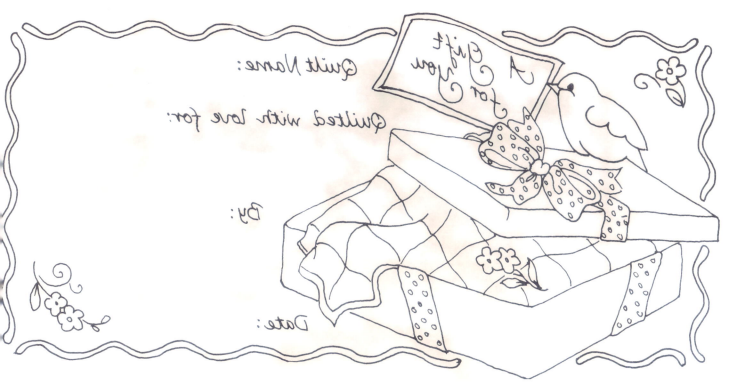

Test Transfer

For A
Special
Girl

Date:

To:

With love from:

Friends and Quilts are a great source of comfort

Quilt Name:

Made by:

Date:

26

Test Transfer

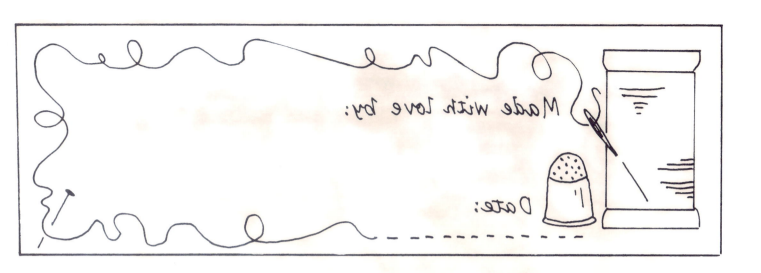

Made with love by:

Date:

Quilting Angel

Quilt Name

Made by

Date

Test Transfer

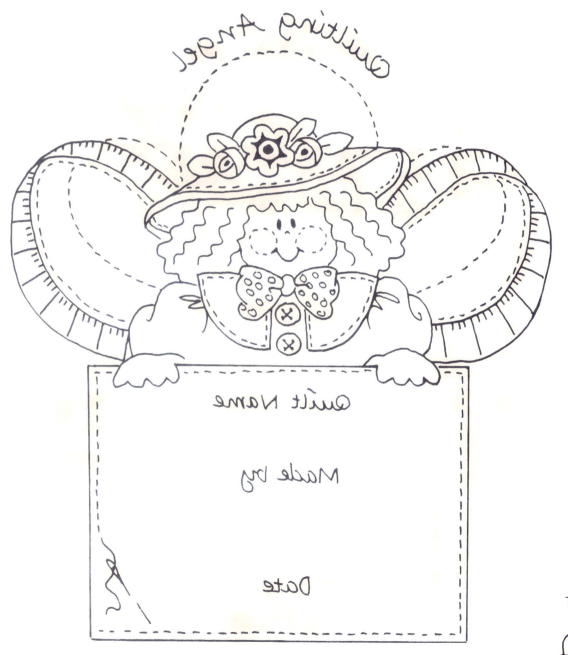

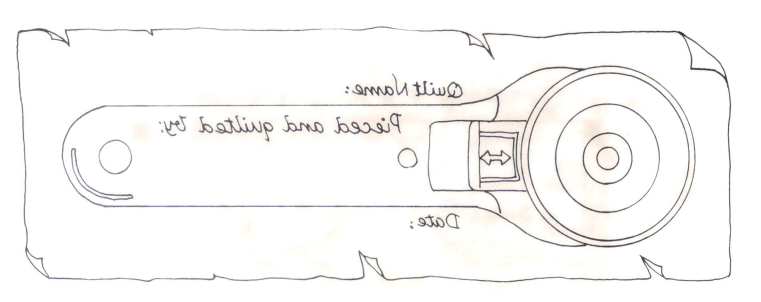

Quilt Name:

Pieced and quilted by:

Date:

Quilt Name:

Appliqued with love by:

Date:

Test Transfer

28

Friendship is a slow-growing flower

Quilt Name:

Made especially for:

Made by:

Date:

Test Transfer

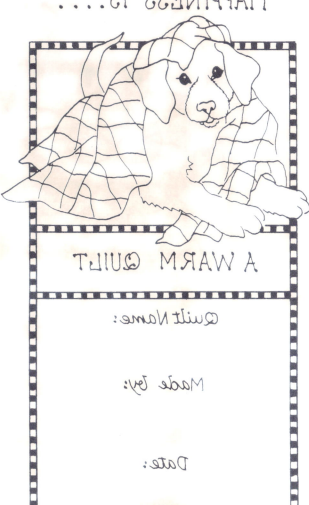

HAPPINESS IS.....

A WARM QUILT

Quilt Name:

Made by:

Date:

Quilts and friends add color to life.

A friendship quilt for:

Made by:

Date:

Test Transfer

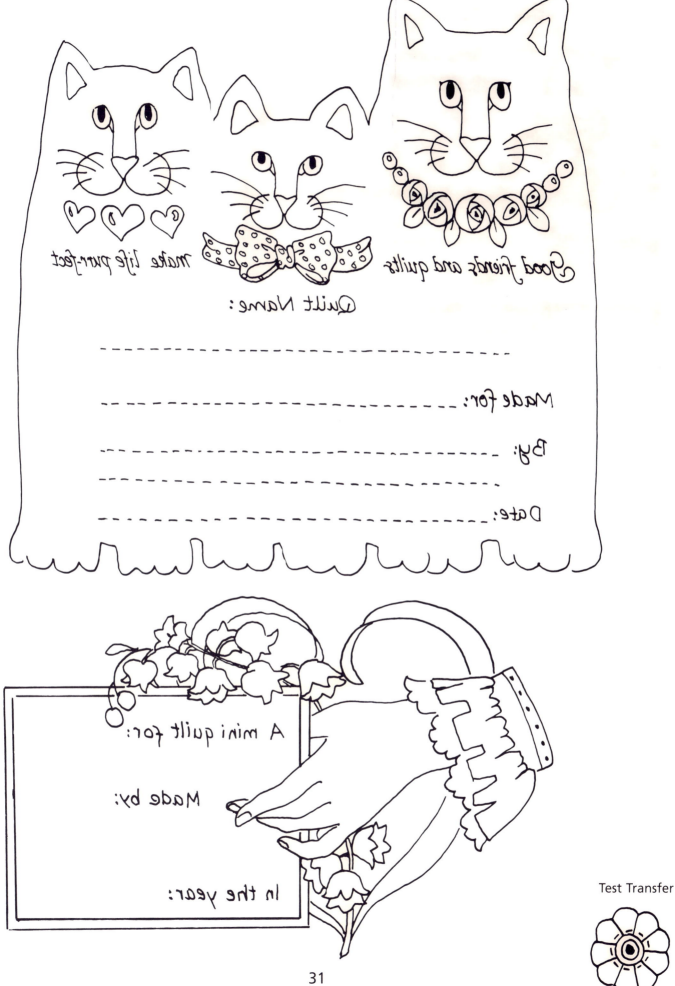

Good Friends and quilts

make life purr-fect

Quilt Name:

Made for:

By:

Date:

A mini quilt for:

Made by:

In the year:

Test Transfer

31

Finishing and Attaching Your Label

Use the fine-point marker to record label information in your own handwriting or trace the letters from the alphabet provided. Lay your label over the desired letters and use the fine-point permanent marker to trace the letters onto the label.

Leaving ½" on all sides for turning under the raw edges, trim label as desired. Press under raw edges and blindstitch label to the back of your quilt. For a more decorative finish, try sewing lace trim, ribbon, or rickrack around the label or add buttons to the corners.

Life is a quilt sewn together with memories.

Quilt Name:
Rainbow Bright
Pieced and quilted by:
by Maria Rodriguez
for Tom Parrish
On our wedding
Date: 2006

A a B b C c D d E e F f G g H h I i J j K k L l M m

N n O o P p Q q R r S s T t U u V v W w X x Y y Z z

1 2 3 4 5 6 7 8 9 0

A a B b C c D d E e F f G g H h I i J j K k L l M m

N n O o P p Q q R r S s T t U u V v W w X x Y y Z z

1 2 3 4 5 6 7 8 9 0

Embroidery Stitches

Backstitch

Come up at 1, go down at 2, and come up at 3 (Fig. 1). Continue working as shown in Fig. 2. Length of stitches may be varied as desired.

Fig. 1

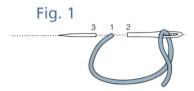

Fig. 2

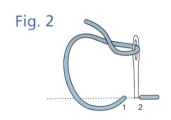

French Knot

Follow Figs. 3 – 6 to complete French Knots. Come up at 1. Wrap thread twice around needle and insert needle at 2, holding end of thread with non-stitching fingers. Tighten knot; then pull needle through, holding floss until it must be released. For larger knot, use more strands; wrap only once.

Fig. 3

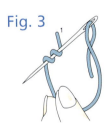

Fig. 4

Fig. 5

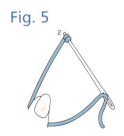

Fig. 6

Lazy Daisy Stitch

Bring needle up at 1; take needle down again at 1 but not in the same hole to form a loop; bring needle up at 2. Keeping loop below point of needle (Fig. 7), take needle down at 3 to anchor loop (Fig. 8).

Fig. 7

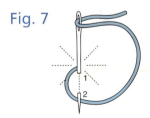

Fig. 8

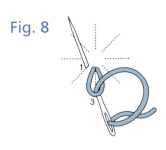

Running Stitch

The running stitch consists of a series of straight stitches with the stitch length equal to the space between stitches (Fig. 9).

Fig. 9

Satin Stitch

Come up at 1. Go down at 2, and come up at 3. Continue until area is filled (Fig. 10).

Fig. 10

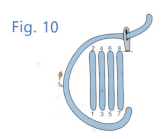

Stem Stitch

Come up at 1. Keeping thread below stitching line, go down at 2 and come up at 3. Go down at 4 and come up at 5 (Fig. 11).

Fig. 11

Straight Stitch

Bring needle up at 1 and take needle down at 2 (Fig. 12). Length of stitches may be varied as desired.

Fig. 12

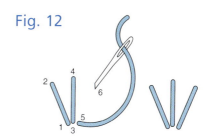

A
friendship
quilt
from all of us
- - - - - - - - - - - - - - - -
To: *Lilly Potter*

With love from:

Bertha Hazel

Katie Leung

Emma Watson

Mitch Stacy

In the year: 2006
In the city and state of:
Concord, California

Production Team
Creative Director — Donna Kooler
Editor-In-Chief — Judy Swager
Graphic Designer — María Rodríguez
Photographer — Dianne Woods
Photo Stylist — Basha Kooler
Editorial Assistant — McKenzie Mortensen
Proofreader — Char Randolph

KOOLER
DESIGN
STUDIO
BOOKS

Produced By: Kooler Design Studio
399 Taylor Blvd., Ste. 104
Pleasant Hill, CA 94523
www.koolerdesign.com

LEISURE
ARTS
the art of everyday living

Notes

_____

_____

_____

_____

_____

_____

_____

_____

_____

_____

_____

_____

_____

_____

_____

_____

_____